Original title:
The Aloe Diaries



Author: Ophelia Ravenscroft

ISBN HARDBACK: 978-1-80581-936-3
ISBN PAPERBACK: 978-1-80581-463-4
ISBN EBOOK: 978-1-80581-936-3

## Whispering Whorls

In my pot, a green diva sits,
Whispers secrets with funny quips.
'Stand tall!' she says, as I brew tea,
'Life's too short to just be me!'

Her fronds are wild, they sway and dance,
Throwing sass in every glance.
'Don't quit me now, let's have some fun,
Not all my days are straight in the sun.'

## Shadows of Serenity

In shadows long, she reclines with glee,
Under the sun, with a sip of brie.
'Life's a joke!' her leaves proclaim,
'Chasing dreams isn't always lame.'

A dance of dust, with jests and jibes,
Charming all with her quirky vibes.
'Stretch out, don't fret, just take a cue,
Who needs a crown? I'm the queen, it's true!'

## The Green Elixir

Promised potions I dare to brew,
With each sip, a chuckle anew.
‘A drop of green might save your day,
Throw worries out, let laughter play.’

Mixing herbs, she stirs with flair,
‘Truth be told, I’m always rare!
Drink up, dear friend, and join the spree,
Life’s like this: funny, wild, carefree!’

## Stories of Survival

Once I swayed in a sunny spot,
Dodging drought, life’s steaming plot.
Whisked away from a hungry gnome,
I laughed aloud, ‘I’ve made my home!’

Through storms and sun, I’ve read the script,
Of funny tales, and pranks well-equipped.
Curled up tight, in a muddy zone,
‘Every day’s a party; I’m never alone!’

## Sunlit Sanctuary

In a pot by the sun so bright,
Lives a plant that’s quite a delight.
With leaves that stretch, oh so proud,
It whispers jokes, a little loud.

Each morning it greets with a grin,
Sipping sunlight like a gin.
It dances when breezes blow,
Saying, 'Watch me steal the show!'

## Heart of the Desert

In the desert, where sand does swirl,
A green friend gives the sun a twirl.
With a punchline as sharp as its spikes,
It shares its secrets, oh what a sight!

Cacti giggle as they bask,
But our hero's up for the task.
'Water me? Please! I prefer a drink,
Of humor, my friend, just think, think, think!'

## Echoes of a Healing Plant

Hear the chuckles in the breeze,
From leaves that wave with such ease.
‘Need a remedy?’ they jest,
‘Just a hug, and you’ll feel blessed!’

With sap that’s sticky, yet so sly,
It claims to heal with a winked eye.
‘Put me on a burn,’ it cries,
‘And watch your troubles say goodbyes!’

## A Journey of Green

On a quest through pots and clay,
Our green friend leads the way.
With each twist, it cracks a joke,
'The more I grow, the more I soak!'

Roads of gravel, sunlit paths,
It laughs at all life's little math.
'How much water? You'll find out!
Just a sprinkle, let's not shout!'

## Thorns and Tenderness

In the garden of laughs, thorns do reside,
Yet with each poke, joy won't subside.
A smile peeks through the prickly veil,
As plants and puns weave a comical tale.

Nature's jesters with purpose so bright,
Aloof and cute, they bring pure delight.
Beneath sharp edges, a soft heart sings,
Laughter is found in the weirdest things.

## Nature’s Artisan

Nature’s own jester, with humor divine,
Crafting joy in each leafy line.
Wit wrapped in green, with smiles all around,
In the silliest spots, laughter is found.

Poking fun at the ways we fuss,
While sipping on sunshine, no need to rush.
With every bloom, there’s a chuckle to share,
For art in the garden is everywhere.

## The Succulent Chronicles

In a land of succulents, tales intertwine,
Each one a character, quirky yet fine.
With spiky humor and shades galore,
Who knew plant life could be such a score?

They gossip in whispers, basking in sun,
Finding the joy in their green, leafy fun.
Sharing secrets, the jokes take flight,
In this charming realm, every day's a delight.

## Dusk of the Desert

As the desert moon winks, the cacti sway,
With stories of sunshine and laughter at play.
The night air giggles, a cool, gentle tease,
While prickly fellows dance in the breeze.

Under the starlight, a comical show,
As shadows blend in a synchronized flow.
A cactus made jokes, while the moon only smiled,
In this wild, funny world, nature's beguiled.

## Lush Landscapes

In the garden where laughter grows,
Aloe plants gossip, nobody knows.
With hats made of leaves and shades so bright,
They dance in the breeze, a curious sight.

The flowers giggle, they chatter with glee,
Sipping the sun like it's warm chamomile tea.
A spiky parade in the afternoon light,
They wiggle and wiggle, oh what a delight!

## Verdant Vitality

In a pot so smug, a green friend resides,
With stories of roots and wild, witty rides.
He brags about water and sunshine's embrace,
Claiming fame as the skin-care ace in the race.

With laughter from leaves and secrets to spill,
He tickles the soil, oh what a thrill!
As neighbors complain of tedious weeds,
Our aloe stands proud, fulfilling its needs!

## The Secret of the Sun

Beneath the warm rays, the aloe does take,
A sunbath so lavish, it's surely no mistake.
With a wink and a giggle, it shares its advice,
'Embrace every moment, just like a slice!'

The sun-baked shenanigans, oh what a view,
Fashioning shades of green, bright and new.
As others get burned, he simply grins wide,
'Life’s better when you’re spiky and fried!'

## Tales of the Thicket

In the thicket of green, a party unfolds,
With tales of the soil and laughter retold.
The cacti are crooning, the blooms join the tune,
A festival, oh my, beneath the bright moon!

With friends made of laughter and roots intertwined,
Each spike tells a story, unique and aligned.
The aloe stands tall, a jester at heart,
In the thicket of life, he plays his fine part!

## Elements of Equilibrium

In the sun, they bask and play,
Aloes stretching day by day.
Their spiky laughs, a quirky show,
Teaching plants how to glow.

With friends like cacti, always near,
They share secrets without fear.
Some say they're tough, but they just tease,
While sipping dew with perfect ease.

When rainfall dances on their leaves,
They giggle, sway, and pull up sleeves.
The balance of fun, they always find,
In nature's chaos, they're well aligned.

## Secrets of the Succulent

Old sages say, ‘Be like a plant,’
But look at them, they laugh and chant.
With secrets tucked in each green fold,
They crave the sun and scorn the cold.

‘I've got a stash of water here,’
Said one to another with great cheer.
They swap their tales of drought and bloom,
And plot to take over the room.

In their world, rules bend and sway,
“Thou shalt not move,” they like to play.
Yet watch them dance when no one’s near,
Beneath the moonlight, full of cheer.

## Chronicles of the Green World

Aloes gather for gossip and glee,
Sharing tales of who drinks the sea.
One says, “I stretched to kiss the sky!”
Another laughs, “I’m too cool to die!”

They boast of sunbathing diva days,
With prickly embraces that always amaze.
“Oh, I can survive without a drop,”
Aloe winks, “and still have the chops!”

Their stories are long, with twists galore,
Of desert hikes and rogue uproar.
In each green heart, a legend grows,
In soft whispers, their laughter flows.

## Embracing Elegance

Elegance draped in shades of green,
Aloe poses, a regal queen.
With leaves that shimmer, oh so bright,
Turning heads in the soft moonlight.

"Is that a new pot? Quite a flair!"
"Why, thank you, darling, just a care!"
Their style is smooth, yet a bit poky,
A touch of chic, but slightly hokey.

When the wind swoops by with a sigh,
They sway with grace, oh my, oh my!
Aloes in a dance, so spry and bold,
Charming all, both young and old.

## Succulent Secrets of a Silent Guardian

In a pot I sit with pride,
Green and spiky, never hide.
Water me just twice a week,
Or I'll burst into a cheeky squeak.

Dusty friends come and say hi,
I just nod, I'm way too shy.
With petals sharp and humor dry,
I'm the plant that won't comply.

My leaves have stories, thick and tall,
Of summer sun and rain that falls.
I smile when they try to groom,
But I prefer my own green room!

So here I am, the leafy sage,
Turning over a new page.
Secrets kept with every spike,
Laughing softly, let me strike!

**Diary of Desert Bloom: Resilience Unfurled**

In sandy lands I take my stand,
With roots that stretch like rubber bands.
Sunshine, laughter, bring it on,
I'm the one who'll be here long!

Clumsy gardener, what a sight,
You forgot me—oh, what a fright!
Yet here I thrive, quite serene,
A tenacious little green machine.

An occasional sip, I don't need much,
Just a bit, and I'm in touch.
I bloom in colors, bright and bold,
A story of toughness, to be told.

Watch me dance in the warm sun's glow,
While you panic—Oh no, where'd it go?
I'm resilient, that's my game,
Flourishing bright, never the same!

## Echoes of the Lush: A Plant's Perspective

Oh, look at them rushing about,
I'm just here, without a doubt.
Photosynthesizing with glee,
What a funny sight to see!

I watch the humans chat and sway,
They think they know the plants' way.
But hush now, the secret's clear—
We're just faking interest, my dear!

Leaves whisper tales of weather fine,
And yet they complain about the time.
I soak up sun, while they all fret,
Forgetting I'm the biggest asset!

So take a seat, enjoy the show,
Without us, where would you go?
We're the silent watchers from the pot,
Charming you all, it's what we've got!

**Verdant Chronicles in Windowed Light**

In sunlight's glow, I make my mark,
With leaves like fingers, reaching stark.
I peep out, just a little shy,
As sunlight paints the morning sky.

Photosynthesizing like a pro,
While you complain, 'Where did time go?'
I chuckle in the corner up high,
Nothing beats a plant-life spy!

Got my roots deep in this place,
Watching you run your endless race.
But worry not, I'm here to stay,
Sending smiles throughout the day!

So sip your tea and take a break,
Trust me, it's just what we make.
A world of green, so lively and bright,
In windowed light, we hold the sight!

## Cacti and Companionship

In a pot so snug and tight,
Cacti laugh under the light.
With prickles sharp, they tell their tale,
Of leafy friends who never fail.

One sways with a quirky dance,
While another takes a silly chance.
They poke each other with delight,
A spiky crew, a charming sight.

Each flower blooms, a burst of cheer,
Brightening up their little sphere.
With nature's wit, they bumble along,
In a world where they all belong.

Oh, who needs a bloom so grand?
When you have friends, just take a stand!
With laughter that never seems to fade,
In tiny pots, their fun is made.

## Fronds of Fortune

Beneath the sun, the fronds do sway,
Lucky leaves make up their play.
In greens and golds, they plot and scheme,
Creating mischief like a dream.

One frond whispers to the vine,
"Let's prank the one who said we're fine!"
And with a wiggle, they conspire,
To make a scene that might backfire.

They throw a shade on passing bees,
Who buzz around with woes and pleas.
"Is this a garden, or a circus show?"
The flowers smirk, as laughter flows.

But when the wind comes to play,
All fronds unite in a wild ballet.
With giggles loud in the fragrant air,
They dance and twirl without a care.

## Nature's Emissary

A curious sprout peeks from the ground,
With leafy letters, it makes a sound.
“Dear humans, let’s have some fun!
Join me, before the day is done!”

It wrote a message on a bloom,
“Embrace the spores, dispel the gloom!”
With roots that stretch far and wide,
It calls all creatures to its side.

Frogs croaked loudly, birds took flight,
Together they painted the sky so bright.
A party formed in the forest deep,
While tiny ants marched, non-stop, no sleep.

With twirling vines and dancing leaves,
Nature’s emissary never leaves.
It spreads a cheer that knows no bounds,
In every corner, laughter resounds!

## The Quiet Bloom

In a corner, shy and meek,
A bloom unique, it does not speak.
But oh, when laughter fills the air,
It sways in rhythm, without a care.

With petals soft, it turns to see,
The antics of the buzzing bee.
"Why can't I have such lively zest?"
It wonders, feeling quite compressed.

Then one fine day, with sun so warm,
It felt a tickle, a sudden charm.
With petals fluttering in a breeze,
It joined the fun with playful ease.

Now when the garden fills with glee,
The quiet bloom is full of spree.
What once was shy is now a goof,
In laughter's arms, it found its proof.

## Nectar of the Earth

Beneath the sun, I sway and grin,
My spiky leaves, a joyful spin.
A drop of juice, oh what a treat,
For thirsty bees, I feel so sweet.

With every sip, they dance and cheer,
Their buzzing tunes, music I hear.
I'm not just green; I'm quite a star,
Around this garden, they know who we are.

Another drink! They find me grand,
They love my nectar, it's just so bland!
Not meant for tea or fancy meals,
But on my leaves, that laughter peels.

From pot to pot, I'm on the roam,
An aloe with a funny bone.
I'll always crack a silly joke,
Who knew I'd be the garden's cloak?

## Resilient Roots

Underneath, I hold my ground,
With snickers that are rarely found.
My roots stretch wide, they love to play,
In every drought, I thrive away.

When storms brew up, I just stand tough,
I chuckle at the kind of rough.
Not easy to break, I’m quite the spy,
Aloe's got secrets, oh my, oh my!

With every twist, I make a scene,
A little sassy, slightly green.
I wave my limbs, so high and proud,
Letting the world know 'I’m part of the crowd!'

Just here for laughs, not for despair,
Waving all my worries, done with cares.
Roots in the soil, no need for flight,
In drought or rain, I find the light.

## Memories in the Moisture

Water drips, I catch the drops,
Storing tales in tiny flops.
Every sprinkle, a memory made,
Of laughing friends in sunlight played.

I soak it in, like gossip shared,
A secret keeper, always prepared.
From potting soil to sunny skies,
My moisture swirls with happy sighs.

In every bead, a drop of cheer,
Replays the laughter echoed near.
Spritzing tales of summers past,
With every mist, the fun will last!

I'm the keeper of smiles so bright,
Memories moist, the purest delight.
In laughter's glow, I stand tall,
Catch a hug or two, I'll take them all!

**Blooming in Silence**

In the corner, I sit and wait,
Quietly plotting my plant-based fate.
Not noisy blooms, but colorful frill,
Popping out softly, like a bread roll thrill.

With colors shy, I bring delight,
My blooms know better than show-off might.
In silence I shine, with a wink to the day,
Who said plants can’t laugh or play?

I blossom slowly, a whisper to air,
Not here for glory or show-off flair.
When nobody's watching, I take my chance,
And send out my scent for a secret dance.

In the peace of twilight, I finally sing,
With petals aglow, I am the spring.
Blooming in silence, a joyful sight,
Carrying laughter into the night.

## Hidden Resilience

In pots they sit, so sly and neat,
With spiky hair that can't be beat.
They laugh at drought with a cheeky grin,
Who knew survival could be a win?

When friends stop by and water flows,
They shake their heads, they strike a pose.
These leafy jokers, so chill and bright,
No need for fuss, they're out of sight!

With sunshine streaming, they bask and sway,
Who needs a spa when you're here to play?
An afternoon spent in summer's glow,
Tales of resilience they happily show.

So raise a glass to these green delight,
With humor thick and spirits light.
Cheers to the crown of the desert throne,
For in their wit, we're never alone!

## The Botanist's Journal

In garden beds where secrets creep,
I jot down notes, while others sleep.
Each sprout a giggle, each leaf a jest,
Nature's humor, oh how it's blessed!

A cactus winks, with attitude bold,
"Water me? Ha! I'm quite behold!"
Budding flowers, in petal gowns,
They're plotting pranks to fool the towns.

"Don't trust the weeds!" they softly chime,
They're after sunlight, and that's a crime!
In every sprig, a punchline hides,
While I take notes, the humor rides.

Oh botanist life, a comedy scene,
In spades and trowels, where jokes stay clean.
So flip the pages of this green book,
A merry tale, come take a look!

## Guardian of the Desert

Stuck in sand, with style and flair,
A desert guardian with spiky hair.
“Fear not, my friends!” it seems to say,
“Thrive in the heat; let’s dance and play!”

With roots so deep, it won’t distress,
A watchful eye in nature's dress.
It holds the tales of sun and moon,
In whispers soft, a gentle tune.

“Bring on the storms!” it shouts with glee,
“I'm made for this! Come, dance with me!”
Through gusts and glares, it shakes its spine,
A seasoned vet, forever fine.

So here’s to the guardian, bold and bright,
With humor rich, a true delight.
In every prick and every bloom,
The joy of deserts starts to zoom!

## Elixirs in Everyday Life

In kitchens bright with jars in sight,
Homemade brews that spark delight.
From leafy greens to sunny cheer,
Potions giggle as they disappear.

“Just a pinch!” I say with glee,
This sprinkle of green will set you free!
A dash of zest, a swirl of fun,
Who knew health could feel like sun?

With every sip, a playful laugh,
These potions bring out the inner craft.
Ginger, mint, with a hint of rhyme,
Elixirs forged in pots divine.

So raise your glass, let laughter ring,
In every gulp, the joy we bring.
Life's a garden, and we’re the bees,
Buzzing through life, oh, how it frees!

## Nature's Apothecary

In the garden, greens abound,
A quirky plant spins round and round.
With leaves like swords, it stands so bright,
Giving sunburns quite a fright!

Grew it for smoothies, what a goof!
Turns out, it’s best on my sunburned roof.
A sip of green was more of a flop,
Now it’s a balm, oh, what a swap!

Nature's charm, a blend of laughs,
Holding secrets of plant-based crafts.
With every poke and every nip,
Out of the pot, it starts to slip!

Friends ask me, “What’s that odd leaf?”
I respond with joy, not disbelief.
My prickly friend brings fun galore,
In this gardening game, I’ll explore more!

## The Aloe's Gift

Aloe’s gift, a funny tale,
Grew it tall, it started to sail.
With a wink and a quirky flare,
It took a dive into my hair!

Thought it would cure that dry old spot,
But instead, it gave me quite a plot.
Stuck in my brush, oh what a fright,
Gloopy leaves in morning light!

Plant itself, a comedy show,
Who knew it had quite a flow?
Slapas, drips, and merry slips,
Aloe’s fun, forget the chips!

So here’s to my leafy friend so bold,
With tales of laughter, never old.
In kitchens and baths, it finds its way,
What a crazy plant to brighten the day!

## Artistry in Aloe

Behold my garden, art on display,
Aloe struts in a sassy way.
Leaves like paintbrushes, wielded with glee,
Dancing around, oh look at me!

They say, “Create, bring joy, bring cheer,”
But aloe just winks as if to sneer.
With slathers of goop and a comic twist,
My masterpiece was far from the list!

Mixing potions and crafting charms,
Aloe’s humor brings all the warms.
Painted faces, masking fun,
Who knew a plant could weigh a ton?

Bottles line the counter, think I've gone mad,
But every concoction makes me glad.
So here's to the art, a sticky delight,
With sprinklings of giggles, it feels just right!

## Radiance of Resilience

Oh, resilience, meet the green,
Aloe’s bright, it’s quite the scene.
Through every mishap, it stands so firm,
With a goofy attitude, it’ll always squirm!

Pots may droop, and skies may frown,
But this little plant won’t go down.
With a cheeky grin, it laughs at fate,
“The sun's my buddy, we’re never late!”

I tried to trim just one little leaf,
But oh dear, what a comic grief!
A hundred more sprouts, it must have planned,
“It’s a party! Join in, lend a hand!”

So here’s to the strength in every inch,
Aloe’s telling us to never flinch.
With laughter flowing, it takes the crown,
Resilience rules in this silly town!

## Echoing Growth: The Untold Stories

In a pot I sit so still,
Dreaming of a sunny thrill.
Stretch my leaves to catch the sun,
Looking for the ultimate fun.

My friends in clay, we laugh and grow,
Comparing shades, from dark to glow.
We gossip 'bout the gardener's care,
And plot our leaves in a well-stacked layer.

When the rain does come to play,
We dance like crazy, hip-hip-hooray!
With every drop, our joy expands,
We revel in the moisture's hands.

Oh those who think we're just decor,
Have never seen us on the floor!
Our tales spill out of every seam,
A plant's life is more than a dream!

## Shadows of Growth: A Succulent's Soliloquy

Underneath the table's edge,
We plot our escape, make a pledge.
To sneak about when Owner's gone,
And dance beneath the veil of dawn.

We whisper tales of sunlit days,
Of kitchen scraps and crazy plays.
Everyone thinks we just sit tight,
But oh, the mischief in the night!

A drop of water, a gentle spritz,
Turns us into little hit-or-miss.
Sipping sunbeams, we laugh aloud,
Feeling fancy, standing proud.

So think again, dear friend of green,
We're more than pots—what a scene!
In shadows cast, our hearts ignites,
A succulent's life is pure delights!

**In the Heart of Potting Soil: Green Narratives**

Deep in the soil, we have our chats,
About the big world, and where it's at.
From rocks to roots, we trade our tales,
In our earthy home, the fun never pales.

A worm winks by, and off we giggle,
He loves to wriggle, what a riddle!
Together we grow, no room for fear,
In our cozy pot, we fill with cheer.

Each chip of dirt holds a memory,
Of the sun, the rain, sweet revelry.
With laughter echoed in far-off lands,
Our leafy hearts make dazzling strands.

If you could hear our secret plots,
You'd join us, forget all your knots.
In the art of potting, we find our song,
In soil so rich, we all belong!

## Echoes of Light: A Succulent's Take

Sunshine trickles through the glass,
A golden kiss, a moment’s pass.
We stretch our leaves, a happy sight,
In this dance of warmth and light.

With every glow, we sway and cheer,
Giddy plants, we have no fear.
Our roots are snug, we won't take flight,
Just bask and giggle in delight.

But when the shade brings a surprise,
Oh, the drama in our eyes!
Should we huddle or spread wide?
A succulent’s woe, oh what a ride!

Yet through it all, we find our way,
With jokey roots, come what may.
In this garden's playful tease,
We navigate our joys with ease!

## Embrace of the Aloe

In my garden, green and bright,
My aloe plant gives me a fright.
Its arms reach out, a silly dance,
How did it end up in my pants?

I thought it was just a friend,
Until its spikes began to bend.
With hugs so prickly, oh so bold,
I guess this friendship's getting old!

I tell it jokes, a comic's flair,
It sits there quietly, without a care.
Yet every time I toss a pun,
It seems to laugh, then leaves me stunned!

So here we are, a pair of clowns,
Me in laughter, it in frowns.
If plants could giggle, I would yell,
My aloe's jokes would raise the swell!

## Wisdom of the Waxy

Aloe wise, with wisdom packed,
In its cool gel, no act is cracked.
It’s seen my blunders, all the falls,
Yet never spills my secrets, at all.

With layers thick, it’s quite profound,
A guru of the garden ground.
It speaks in silence, oh so sly,
While I just wonder, ‘Is that a lie?’

What tales of love it could have told,
Of suns too bright and nights too cold.
It's seen my skin turn red like fire,
Yet kindly mutes my wildest desire.

So if you seek a sage in green,
Don’t overlook the plant unseen.
For wisdom lies in every leaf,
Just ask my aloe—then hold your grief!

## Healing Waters

Aloe juice, oh what a treat,
Cooler than ice in summer heat.
I sip and slurp, what a delight,
But why does it wiggle in the light?

I reach for solace in a glass,
But every gulp feels like a pass.
Does it heal? Or does it play?
I'm feeling better, hip hip hooray!

It's rumored to fix every ache,
But tries to swim, oh for goodness' sake!
I pour it out—what a messy role,
Did it just gurgle, or save my soul?

With every drink, I chase the fun,
Aloe's tricks, oh they never shun.
So here's to healing in every sip,
And letting the silly vibes just rip!

**Patterns of Growth**

Aloe grows in wavy lines,
Like tangled thoughts from busy minds.
Each leaf a story, some quite bizarre,
I wonder if it dreams of far?

In perfect rows, they stretch and sway,
Awkwardly, in their own ballet.
One little leaf stands up so tall,
I cheer it on—'You can have it all!'

They twist and turn, a leafy show,
Who knew they had the moves, you know?
A dance-off? Oh, I take my stand,
But alas, I'm just a clumsy hand!

So here's to growth, in weirdest ways,
Laughing with every silly phase.
For in this garden, jokes abound,
With each green sprout, joy can be found!

## Fragments of Terra: Moments in Green

In pots they sit with smug delight,
Daring the sun to pick a fight.
Leaves like hands at a dance-off,
Wobbling, so proud, in their own soft cloth.

I watered one, it gave a shiver,
Claiming drought like a thirsty river.
With each splash, a hiss, a cheer,
“More water, please, it’s not for fear!”

Instead of growing nice and tall,
They wobble, giggle, and nearly fall.
Roots in a twist like a grapevine,
“Oh look! I’m a plant, oh so divine!”

In our homes, these greens take flight,
Sipping sunlight, oh what a sight!
A family of laughs, a comedy crew,
With puns and leaves, they blossom anew.

## A Life Unfurling: Stories of Succulents

In a pot, a story unfolds,
With shivering leaves and hearts made of gold.
One squints at the moon, unsure of the rules,
While others swap tales like eager fools.

They barter for sunlight, a wacky swap,
"Give us your rays, we'll make you non-stop!"
With roots all tangled, a dramatic plight,
Flashing their greens in the soft twilight.

One leaf quips, "I'm practically a star!
With my succulent charm, you'll go very far!"
They shake in laughter, the joystick gang,
"Sipping on jokes, let the fun times clang!"

Competitions held, each plant a tightrope,
Wobbling and laughing, their chronic hope.
From tiny sprigs to a garden rave,
These quirky greens, oh how they behave!

## Gentle Nurturing in a Concrete Jungle

Amidst the gray, they sprout with flair,
A posh little club, with no room to spare.
Each leaf a pillow, each thorn a jest,
Living it up in their leafy nest.

Sunlight filters, a warm embrace,
Watching them grow, with joy on my face.
A sip of the drought while dodging the rains,
In this wild jungle, their humor remains.

“Are we fussy?” laughs the tall, sassy plant,
“Please, bring your water,” they say with a chant.
Decked in green, from top to floor,
They giggle at gardeners, craving for more.

The city’s concrete, a backdrop to jest,
These fun-loving greens put patience to test.
Each day a thrill, each pot a glee,
In this concrete jungle, it’s a plant’s jubilee!

## Sun-Drenched Tales of Thirst and Flourish

Under the sun, they lounge and sip,
Crafting wild stories with each little quip.
Cactus in shades, oh what a sight,
Telling tales of thirst through day and night.

“Who needs a drink?” they jest with a grin,
“Just soak up the rays, let the fun begin!”
From spiky to smooth, character galore,
Each telling a tale like we’ve never heard before.

Dancing in pots, the leaves take flight,
A directly dramatic succulent night.
Drinking the sun, while giggling at clouds,
Filled with stories, they’re eternally proud.

Then comes a shadow, a whispered hue,
“Oh no, our party is getting askew!”
But hey, they shrug it, “We still have our fun,
In the bright beams of laughter, we’ve already won!”

## Beneath the Surface

In the pot, green stalks stand tall,
Whispering secrets of nature's call.
Roots are tangled, a messy affair,
They plot and plan without a care.

Neighbors gossip, the daisies tease,
"Look at those leaves, swaying in the breeze!"
But little do they know their fate,
Aloe's got tricks; just wait, just wait!

Sunshine smiles, they bask in light,
Unaware they're the stars of the night.
Vying for glory, they keep it real,
Those cool green troops, full of zeal!

Beneath the surface, they wiggle and dance,
Teasing the cacti, “Give us a chance!”
In this garden of joy, laughter takes flight,
Aloe and friends, what a delightful sight!

## Healing Hands of Nature

Hands in the soil, muddy and bright,
Tending to plants, oh what a sight!
Poking and prodding, a playful spree,
Sassy succulents giggle with glee.

They say, “We’re magic, don’t you see?
Rub us on sunburns, good as can be!”
Nature's band-aids, on standby they sit,
Healing with humor, a perfect fit.

Dodging the pests like a game of tag,
“Not today, critters, go on, lag!”
With each tiny victory, they brag and boast,
These green little healers, we love the most!

So raise your hands, let’s give a cheer,
To the healing hands that bring us near.
Nature’s remedies, full of style,
With aloe around, we’re sure to smile!

## Tales of Transformation

Once a pup, just a little sprout,
Grew into glory, with a twist and a shout.
Neighbors watched, their eyes open wide,
As Aloe strutted, full of pride.

"Look at me now!" it would proudly say,
"From humble beginnings, I've paved my way!"
Armfuls of moisture, a silky green sheen,
Making transformations fit for a queen.

Sharing stories of sweet delight,
Turning sunburns to smiles, oh what a sight!
With each passing day, a change unfolds,
Aloe, the icon, brave and bold.

Every leaf a chapter, every sip a tale,
Of giggles and growth, beyond the veil.
So gather around, lend me your ear,
For stories of Aloe that bring us cheer!

## Serenity in Succulence

In a world full of chaos, take a pause,
Succulents giggle, and so should you, because
Their plump little bodies, so calm and cool,
Whisper peace secrets, a wise little school.

Breathe in the joy, let stress slip away,
Aloe's here to brighten your day.
A gentle reminder to take it slow,
In their leafy embrace, let worries go.

In hues of green, a tranquil scene,
They sway lightly, serene and keen.
With laughter around, the vibe's just right,
Even the thorns chuckle, what a delight!

So step into the garden, let laughter reign,
With goblins of green that soothe any pain.
Serenity blooms where succulents thrive,
In the laughter of leaves, we feel so alive!

## Echoes in the Embers

In the shack of sunny bliss,
Aloe plants all dance and twist.
With soil on their leafy hats,
Wondering where the sunshine's at.

Their neighbors – cacti, stiff and bold,
Claim ownership of stories told.
But Aloe giggles in the sun,
Wishing for a water gun!

Each night they share some gossip cheer,
Of how their leaves will persevere.
Though spiky friends are sharp in stance,
Aloe just wants to learn to prance.

With every droplet that they sip,
They plan a silly field trip.
To sunbathe on a windowsill,
Or join the worms on a wild thrill!

## Fortitude in Fragility

Tiny leaves with mighty dreams,
Dancing softly in sunlit beams.
They stand tall with gentle grace,
In every corner, they find space.

When raindrops come, they twirl and shout,
'We're not scared! Come on, let's pout!'
With roots like rubber, firm and wide,
They sway and bend with funky pride.

In moments when the wind does blow,
They bend and giggle, 'Look at us go!'
For every gust that comes their way,
They laugh, 'Survival's just a play!'

With whispers soft and colors bright,
They write a tale in pure delight.
For in this fragile, leafy space,
They find their strength in every trace.

## Roots of Resilience

Deep beneath, the roots do spread,
While above, they make silly threads.
In whispering soils, secrets grow,
Messy tales of high and low.

Aloe’s roots embrace each crack,
Sipping juice from nature's sack.
With every storm and sunny ray,
They cheer, 'We’ll always find a way!'

In neighbors’ shade, they laugh and jest,
While shrugging off the heavy fest.
In this jungle, wild and vast,
They find their joy that ever lasts.

And when the night begins to fall,
They giggle as the shadows call.
For in the dark, their spirits beam,
As they share the wackiest dream!

## Whispers of Wellness

In quiet corners, echoes chime,
Aloe makes the silliest rhyme.
With laughter tucked beneath their spines,
They tickle roots with joyful lines.

They soak up sun and drink up mood,
While flourishing in happiness food.
With every laugh, they share a cheer,
‘We’re the best, loud and clear!’

In every droplet, wellness glows,
Their funny antics, how it flows!
They giggle in a sunny stew,
Finding joy in what they do.

So here's to leaves with zest and zeal,
Their twisted tales are truly real.
With humor shining in their space,
They make this world a happier place!

## Whispering Leaves

In sunlit corners, secrets lie,
Aloes gossip with the sky.
They chuckle softly, sway with glee,
Sharing tales of yesterday's bee.

With every breeze, a silly shout,
Their laughter blooms, there's no doubt.
In potted homes, they dance and sway,
Making dull moments a fun play.

## Green Guardians

Upright sentinels, bold and bright,
Keeping watch throughout the night.
With prickly arms that tease and poke,
Who knew plants could crack such jokes?

They guard the shelves with silly grace,
Chasing shadows in their space.
An aloe's wink, a funny spark,
A lush life lived, with a playful mark.

## Stories from a Silent Succulent

Aloe's quiet, but oh so wise,
With secrets hidden in its eyes.
Whispered tales of deserts vast,
In sandy homes, they grow so fast.

They've seen the sun, they’ve felt the rain,
Each leaf a story, joy or pain.
Yet in their stillness, laughter sings,
Picking puns from prickly things.

## Resilience in Every Leaf

Though storms may come and winds may blow,
This plant stands firm, with an inner glow.
A twist and bend, oh what a sight,
It laughs at life, always light.

With every bruise, it tells a jest,
“To thrive is fun, just be the best!”
A little green with lots of cheer,
Aloe's wisdom drawn so clear.

## From Sand to Soil: Chronicles of Adaptation

In the desert, I did dwell,
Sandy jokes, I know so well.
Waving cacti, giving a grin,
Wondering where my water's been.

Blowing breezes, tickling leaves,
Sandy brothers, no one grieves.
Rooting deeper, feeling bold,
Tales of sunburn, never told.

I sipped the sun, oh so sweet,
Now I'm thriving, can't be beat.
Funky friends in droughts we share,
Making laughter, everywhere.

The sands of time shift and swirl,
In this dance, we laugh and twirl.
Adapt and grow, life's little jest,
In this soil, I feel the best.

## A Chlorophyll Chronicle: Tales of Survival

Green and growing, what a sight,
Photosynthesis, my delight.
Chlorophyll, my secret friend,
Turning sunlight, I transcend.

Dancing leaves sway with the breeze,
Sipping laughter, just like peas.
Shady tales in the bright sun,
Why can’t this day be more fun?

Competing with the leafy crew,
Witty plants, they know what to do.
Jokes about the growing pains,
Laughing hard in sunny lanes.

Sassy vines with tales to weave,
Joining forces, we believe.
Life’s a garden, dig it right,
Sprouting joy, a pure delight.

## Beneath the Surface: Life Beneath the Soil

Down below, where roots entwine,
Earthen secrets, oh so fine.
Wiggly worms with silly grins,
Telling tales where life begins.

Rats and critters scurry near,
Moles with jokes, don't shed a tear.
Tickling fungi, spongy and round,
Laughing softly beneath the ground.

Mud pies made in rainy weather,
Shoveling dirt, what fun together!
In the gloom, we thrive and cheer,
Underground, we've got no fear.

Roots and rhymes in cozy nooks,
Reading tales, like open books.
Life's a giggle, down below,
Join the dance, come on, let's go!

## Soothing Succulence

Plump and juicy, that’s my style,
Waddling round with the utmost smile.
Succulent tales, so sweet and bright,
Filling hearts with pure delight.

Rub me gently, take your time,
I’ll come back with antics sublime.
Water me once, let’s not be hasty,
This slow life, it’s oh so tasty!

Spiky laughs, they really sting,
But this charm, it’s what I bring.
Life’s a succulent kind of tease,
Growing proud in the warmest breeze.

With every sip, I bloom with glee,
Sharing secrets, just you and me.
Laughter bubbles, sweet and fine,
In this green world, we gladly shine.

## Tales from the Trough

In the garden, oh what a sight,
Aloe plants chuckle with delight.
They gossip and giggle, all in jest,
About the weeds who never rest.

One says, 'Look at that pesky crab!'
'He thinks he's cool, but he's just a fab!'
'With his crooked stance and patchy leaves,'
'They seem to think they're meant to please.'

## Prickly Embrace

Aloe hugs are not for the meek,
With spiky tendrils, oh so unique.
'Come closer,' they say with a mischievous grin,
But one wrong move, and oh, the sting!

'They bring the warmth, but fail the cuddle,'
Said the poor cactus stuck in a muddle.
'At least they're green and somewhat spry,
But my dear, these hugs? I’d rather fly!'

## A Leaf's Lament

Oh, to be a leaf, one sunny day,
But the sun's too hot, can't I just play?
With the breeze a-whooshing, life feels grand,
Till the gardener shows up, with shovel in hand!

'Whose bright idea was it to grow here?'
I quiver and shake, oh dear, oh dear!
They’ll slice and they’ll dice, I’ll be a salad soon,
Next time, I’ll sprout under the moon!

## Guardian of the Garden

Aloes stand tall, with pride on their face,
Guarding the flowers, in this lovely space.
'Keep your distance, pesky bugs!' they chant,
'Or you'll be in trouble, just like that plant.'

With their spiky shields, they raise a cheer,
'We'll win this battle, the coast is clear!'
So next time you stroll past this plant brigade,
Just remember the humor in the prickly parade!

## Thorns of Wisdom: Lessons from Leaf

In a pot on the sill, I sit with glee,
My prickly persona, who could disagree?
You think I'm all tough, a stone-cold case,
But inside I'm soft, with a warm embrace.

When life's a desert, and you've no clue,
Just lean on my wisdom, it'll guide you through.
Don't fear the poke, it's just my style,
A little sharp humor goes a long mile!

Water me not, I prefer dry air,
A lesson in limits, life's lesson rare.
I stand tall and proud, with my quirky flair,
Just remember dear friend, I'm always there.

So when you're in doubt, just gaze at me,
With laughter and wit, together we'll be.
In thorns, I find fun, in green, I find cheer,
Let's dance with the sun, harvest smiles here!

## Conversations with a Green Companion

Oh, dear little friend, with your leaves so bright,
What's the gossip today? What's the latest plight?
You say you've been drooping, feeling quite blue,
Just stretch for the sun, it's waiting for you.

We swap all our tales, of laughter and tears,
Like plants in a pot, we share all our fears.
You say I'm a diva, so sharp and so bold,
But you hide your critters, if truth be told!

With your spiky charm, and my witty chase,
We root for each other in this leafy space.
A friendship that grows, like branches entwined,
In our garden of giggles, true joy we find.

So here's to our chats, you and I, my mate,
In the hustle of life, we refuse to be late.
Let's laugh at the weeds, and dance in the rain,
For this green companionship is never in vain!

## Growth Patterns: A Botanical Memoir

Once a tiny sprout, well, look at me now,
A cactus of knowledge, take that, and how!
With every little poke, and every sharp grin,
I’ve bloomed into wisdom where laughter begins.

Days stretch like shadows, I soak in the sun,
With each drop of water, life's lessons so fun.
You laugh at my thorns, and I’ll laugh right back,
For humor’s my armor, on this green track.

I sway with the breeze, oh, what a delight,
In nature's grand play, every day feels right.
With roots running deep, I can’t help but thrive,
Spreading laughter and joy, keeps the soul alive.

So here’s to my path, a whimsical route,
With laughter and growing, there's never a doubt.
A funky green memoir, sweet laughter we’ll share,
In every little poke, there's joy in the air!

## Nature's Sentinels: Tales of Survival

In the wild's harsh grip, we stand like a team,
Guardians of green, can't burst our dream.
With spiky defenses, our humor intact,
We tackle life's troubles, and that's a fact!

When storms roll in, and the world seems bleak,
We huddle together, our bond remains sleek.
You bring the sunshine, I'll add the zest,
In the garden of life, we both do our best.

With tales of resilience, we laugh through the pain,
Embracing what comes, like a refreshing rain.
Our stories are sown, like seeds in the ground,
In this forest of fun, our spirits are bound.

So here's to survival, with giggles and glee,
A chorus of laughter, come join in with me!
For every thorn poked, there's joy to be shared,
In nature's embrace, we are always prepared!

## Timeless in Tranquility

In a pot, she sits so green,
Not a single day machine.
Sunshine whispers in her ear,
"Stay right here, there's naught to fear!"

Her leaves stretched out, a peaceful fan,
Mimics yoga, oh what a plan!
With a sip of water, she'll gladly cheer,
"Who needs a spa? I'm the diva here!"

Basking in rays, a carefree queen,
Making all the others seem routine.
With every twitch and gentle sway,
She croons a tune: "I'm here to stay!"

Her roots dance deep, a funny sight,
Whispering secrets deep in night.
Neighbors glance with puzzled glee,
"What on earth could plant life be?"

## Dialogues with the Desert

A cactus chuckles at the sun,
"With my spines, I've already won!"
Sandy jokes fly through the heat,
While lizards laugh and scurry their feet.

"Hey, Mr. Lizard, come sit with me!
Tell me your secrets, oh so free."
The lizard blinks, a bit bemused,
"I'm just here to stay amused!"

Underneath the blazing glow,
The wise old rock grins, "Take it slow!"
"Life's a trip, not just a race,
Laughter's key in this arid place."

Together they jest about life's quirks,
While the sun plays peek-a-boo with smirks.
Each sandy grain, a giggle shared,
In their corner, moments are declared.

## Pulse of the Plant

With every drip from pastel blooms,
A plant giggles, dispelling glooms.
"Water's my favorite comedy show,
Watch me thrive, oh don’t you know?"

In a pot with colors bright,
The leaves play tag, what a sight!
Happiness sprouts; can you believe?
Plant life’s more fun than you'd conceive!

“Hey, Bloomer, why’d the gardener sigh?
I don’t know, but it went awry!”
Giggles echo, as petals twirl,
Dancing leaves in a leafy whirl.

Roses blush, and daisies laugh,
In this garden, treasuring the half.
Sunshine rays with laughter swell,
In the giggle of greens, all is well!

## The Fabric of Flora

Threads of green weave tales so grand,
In leafy laughter, the herbs all stand.
“Join the party, don’t be shy!
Botanical fun will never die!”

Petals flutter like crazy fans,
Rustling secrets of zany plans.
“Let’s throw a bash!” shouts out the sprout,
“Under the moon, we'll dance about!”

With sun-kissed laughter, they stitch and sew,
Creating joy wherever they grow.
“Life is but a humorous play,
Let’s giggle through this bright bouquet!”

In the garden’s embrace, where fun intertwines,
A tapestry of antics and playful designs.
Where flowers jest and the breeze spins tales,
In the fabric of flora, merriment prevails!

## Dialogues with the Green

In pots we meet, my leafy friend,
You share your leaves, I share my trend.
You say I'm dry, I laugh aloud,
You hide my snacks beneath your cloud.

We swap our tales of sun and shade,
You sigh of roots, while I parade.
A dance of dirt, a wiggle here,
I fear your thorns, but love your cheer.

You boast of blooms, a flowered crown,
I dream of water when you frown.
We giggle at the gardener's fuss,
As we roll in laughter, just us plus the dust.

In whispers soft, we softly pledge,
To conquer pots along the hedge.
With laughter bright, we twist and bend,
Life's a joke, my prickly friend!

## Keepers of the Sun

Oh dear sun, where art thou shine?
You keep me warm, oh how divine!
But wait, more shade! I beg with glee,
My leaves are crisp, oh woe is me!

You play the game of hide and seek,
A peek-a-boo that leaves me weak.
I call for rain, you tease with glare,
Keepers of sun, oh it's not fair!

With every droplet, I hold my breath,
The warmth of life, but fear of death.
Just one more squeeze, I promise to thrive,
But keep me hydrated, let me survive!

Together we dance, a wobbly waltz,
Sun and succulent, both with faults.
But in this battle, we'll have our fun,
Oh funny fate, keep us in the sun!

## Echoes in the Evergreen

In quiet woods, I hear a shout,
A cactus whispers, with a pout.
“No water here, come take a look!”
I laugh and tease, it’s quite a book!

The ferns roll their eyes, with sass galore,
“Evergreen friends, just ask for more!”
We echo laughter through the leaves,
A chorus full of happy thieves.

As branches sway with leafy glee,
We trade our secrets, just you and me.
In every rustle, a story spins,
In echoes shared, where fun begins!

Oh woodland pals, let’s all unite,
In playful jests, and jokes delight.
Through every sprout and every seed,
We’ll laugh in joy, that’s all we need!

## Sun-Kissed Remedies

A morning brew of sunshine bright,
I sip my tea, oh what a sight!
With leaves of green and charm so sweet,
I laugh at woes, it’s quite a treat!

“Just add some love,” the plants all cheer,
“Your troubles fade, they disappear!”
With every drop of dew I find,
My worries thin, my joy unwind.

A sprinkle here, a douse of cheer,
The sun lifts spirits, never fear!
We gather round, the herbs align,
With blossoms bold, oh how we shine!

In this bright garden, humor blooms,
A remedy found among the fumes.
With giggles shared and roots entwined,
We make new tales, forever kind!

## Nature’s Narrative

In the garden, plants converse,
Aloe says, "You’ve got a curse!"
The cactus grins, "Don't be a bore,"
"I'm spiky but can still explore."

A marigold shares a floral joke,
"Why did the seed take a poke?"
The daisies giggle, petals aflutter,
"It wanted to grow, but fell in the gutter!"

The leaves plot pranks with glee,
"Let's switch places, just wait and see!"
A fern laughs, "You'll be quite lost,"
"But I guess it's worth the cost!"

So in nature, fun thrives anew,
With sly smiles from the leafy crew.
Each plant a character in full bloom,
In this green world, there's never gloom.

## Resilient Realms

In a pot, an aloe stands tall,
"I survived that last frost, how about you all?"
The succulents chuckle, their leaves so bright,
"We thrive in sunshine, we will be alright!"

A rubber plant rolls its glossy eyes,
"You're overachieving, oh what a surprise!"
"I've lost a leaf or two in the fight,"
"But I'm still here, oh, what a sight!"

The herbs sway, unfazed by the heat,
"We'll spice up the world, can't be beat!"
A thyme winks, "Though I'm small, take heed,"
"In this resilient realm, we all take the lead!"

As seasons change, they're quick to adapt,
In their leafy realms, they're all tightly wrapped.
With laughter and strength, they dance in the sun,
In this funny garden, they've all just begun.

## Dusk of the Yucca

In the twilight, a yucca stands proud,
"I'm not a palm, I don't need a crowd!"
The evening breeze whispers with delight,
"Your spiky hair shines in the moonlight!"

A lizard, bright, claims the scene,
"Yucca, you're the sharpest evergreen!"
With a wink, the yucca sways its head,
"I guess I'm just the thorny thread!"

As stars twinkle, shadows play,
A gentle breeze sends the critters away.
"But don't forget, I'm fun and chic!"
"Just watch your step or you might squeak!"

In this dusk, they giggle and play,
A yucca's charm brightens the day.
Nature's laughter rings through the night,
With spiky humor, they take flight.

## The Leaf Whisperer

In the garden, a leaf starts to chat,
"Hey, did you hear about that silly cat?"
The basil replies, all fragrant and green,
"Was it the one that danced with a screen?"

A sunflower bursts out with a grin,
"I heard it twirled like it just couldn't win!"
The thyme giggles, "What a goofy sight,"
"Only in the garden, it can take flight!"

So, with whispers, they share and play,
Creating tales at the end of the day.
"Life’s too short to wilt in despair,"
"Join the fun, if you dare!"

As the sun sets on this leafy affair,
The garden hums with laughter in the air.
Being green and quirky is always a must,
In this vibrant world, it’s a leaf's trust.

## A Tale of Thorns

Once a cactus thought it wise,
To wear a crown of spiky highs.
But when it lost a playful bet,
It pricked itself, oh what a fret!

In the desert, they all gathered round,
To see who'd wear the prickly crown.
But laughter echoed in the air,
As thorns turned pride into despair.

A duel was set, oh what a sight,
With plants all preening, full of fright.
One gusty wind blew off the crown,
Now the cactus sports a frown.

So if you plan to seek some fame,
Remember, thorns can bring you shame.
For in the end, if you're too proud,
You might just end up prickled loud!

## Nature's Solace

In gardens green where laughter grows,
A flower whispered, ‘Life just flows!’
But bees buzzed in with sticky plans,
And soon became the flower’s fans.

A worm rolled by in search of treats,
It wriggled through the soil's beats.
The flower shouted, ‘Mind my stem!’
But worms can’t hear; they’re lost in gem.

They danced around the flower’s roots,
In search of nameless hidden fruits.
With every wiggle, there was cheer,
The garden echoed nature’s sneer.

So when you stroll through blooms and grass,
Remember, some will simply pass.
Laughter sings in nature’s tune,
Even if worms just drool at noon!

**Litanies of the Leaf**

Oh fluttering leaves with tales to share,
In rustling whispers, full of flair.
They've seen the sun play hide and seek,
And once convinced a twig to speak.

A squirrel once tried to scale a tree,
But tangled up in a leafy spree.
The leaves all laughed, they swayed and swirled,
As nutty antics unfurled.

With every gust, a giggle escaped,
As branches danced, the squirrel gaped.
A leaf declared, “Let’s have some fun!
Join in the dance until we’re done!”

So next you see those leaves at play,
Join in the fun, don’t shy away.
For every rustle speaks of cheer,
And nature’s laughter pulls us near!

## Giants of the Garden

In a patch of dirt where giants roam,
A sunflower claimed, “This is my home!”
With petals wide and stems so tall,
It vied for glory, wanting it all.

But oh! A pumpkin rolled by one day,
It giggled loud, “What do you say?
You’ve got the height, but I’ve got the size,
Who’ll win the prize in this garden guise?”

The pair debated, roots intertwined,
As carrots cheered from the sidelines.
The radishes blushed, a little shy,
While beans climbed higher, aiming for the sky.

In the end, they all agreed to play,
To toss their seeds in a merry way.
A garden full of laughs and cheer,
Where even giants have nothing to fear!

www.ingramcontent.com/pod-product-compliance
Lightning Source LLC
Chambersburg PA
CBHW070312120526
44590CB00017B/2646
* 9 7 8 1 8 0 5 8 1 4 6 3 4 *